Star Wars Jokes

Unofficial Jokes for Star Wars Fans

Aaron Stark

D1414651

Star Wars Jokes

What did the Jedi say when someone called him a nerfherder? "Takes one to Obi-wan."

How did Anakin become Darth Vader? He went from Padawan to Bad-awan.

Why wasn't the droid hungry? It already BB-ate.

What kind of animals does What happens if you spend too much money on droids? You go into Boba Debt.

How does Anakin's mom introduce herself? "It's Sh-me!"

What do Senators put in their coffee? Bailey's Organa.

Where does Luke Skywalker play golf? The Course.

What should Leia's neighbors have done when the Death Star showed up? Alder-ran.

How do droids get rid of flies? They say, "R2-D-Shoo."

Who's the most glamorous member of the First Order? General Lux.

Which character in the Office is also in Star Wars? A Jedi Dwight.

How many drinks did the robot want? R2-D-Two.

What's Rey's favorite type of flower? Daisies.

Yes or no, are droids the best? R2-D-True.

Who's the meanest teacher in the Galaxy? Darth Grader.

What did the bounty hunter name his dog? Boba Fetch.

What does the rebellion drink? Jedi Sprite.

What kind of dance moves do storm troopers do? The dark slide.

How did the droid get a piece of cake? It said, "I want one R2-D-Too."

Why does the rebellion only attack after dark? They want to be Jedi Nights.

How do Jedi go ice climbing? With a mind-pick.

What did Mark Hamill name his parrot? Sky-squawker.

What do weird Wookie students do? Chew-chalk-ah.

What do you call someone who does the Kessel Run in 20 parsecs? Slow-da.

Why did Peter Cushing lose his job? They Canned Moff Tarkin.

What does the Resistance drink when they go to the bar? Qui-Gon Gin and Tonic.

What do you call someone who gets a lucky shot in Star Wars? Fluke Skywalker.

What's Han Solo's favorite type of car? A Ford.

Where does Darth Vader go to relax? The Breath Star.

What do Star Wars characters say at rock concerts? "I've got a rad feeling about this."

Why is Daisy Ridley friends with Superman? They both have x-Rey vision.

How did the droid pretend to be a cow? It kept saying, "R2-D-Moo."

How did Han let Chewy know he was ready to date again? He said, "I'm riding Solo."

What does Anakin call a bug on his head? A mind-tick.

What does Natalie Portman sleep in a barn? She's likes the smell of Pad-hay.

How do Jedi eat ice-cream? With mind-licks.

What do you call a rebel that goes vegan? Boss Grass.

What did Anakin wear to a country bar? Plaid-awans.

Why does Darth Vader's dog always go to the bathroom when there's thunder? It's a Storm Pooper.

Why did Anakin follow trends? He liked fad-awans.

How does Carrie Fisher make a cake? With many Leia-ers.

What do you call a member of the resistance who's scared to fight? A Jedi Fright.

How do Jedi build houses? With mind-bricks.

Why did Yoda join the church? He wanted to be a Jedi Pastor.

Why does Anakin need chocolate? He doesn't, he Pada-wants it.

Why didn't Han Solo buy a car? He couldn't Harrison af-ord it.

What do Star Wars characters do in casinos? Make a Boba Bet.

How do Jedi perform comedy? With a mind-schtick.

What do you call a Wookie rapper? Chew-Flocka Flame.

How did the young trainee react to failing his Jedi teest? He was sad-awan.

How do people make fun of the leader of the First Order? They call him "Supreme Leader Joke."

What's Mark Hamill's best sport? Sky-soccer.

Where does a Jedi buy headphones? The Source.

Why is Leia's favorite movie Kung Fu Panda? She likes Po.

What do you call a Sith Lord that joins the rebellion? Darth Traitor.

What would Han Solo use instead of a lightsaber? A Harrison sword.

What do you call two droids who are friends? BB-Mates.

Who has the most books in the galaxy? Read Leader.

What does Natalie Portman's horse say? Pad-neigh.

Which Star Wars character can walk in low water? Darth Wader.

Why did Anakin do such bad things? For Pad-bae.

What does Darth Vader call his family?
"My ana-kin."

Why was Han Solo playing chess on the ship? He was Harrison Bored.

Who defeated Han Solo in Episode V?
A carbon-knight.

What does Ben Solo call his man cave?
The Kylo Den.

What do you call a robot junk dealer?
Bot-O.

What are Luke and Leia? Ana-twins.

What do you call a smart Gungan? Jar Jar Thinks.

How does Daisy Ridley help out her local animal shelter? She feeds the st-Reys.

What would Darth Vader say to Harvey Dent? "I find your lack of face disturbing."

Who serves food on the Death Star? Darth Waiters.

Why do the rebels need bug-spray? To protect from Jedi Bites.

Who takes everything from the pantry in Star Wars? Darth Raider.

What do you call frat boys in Star Wars? Brad-awan and Chad-awan.

What are young people called on the dark side? Palpa-teens.

Where are droids kept at night? In a BB-Crate.

What kind of parties do people throw in Star Wars? Boba Fetes.

What will Mark Hamill sit in when he's old? A Sky-rocker.

What do you call hockey players on the Death Star? Darth Skaters.

What does Han Solo decorate his house with on Thanksgiving? Harrison Gourds.

Where does Mark Hamill keep his stuff at the gym? In a Sky-locker.

What do you call an unlucky Gungan?
Jar Jar Jinx.

What kind of animals do bounty
hunters keep? Boba pets.

Where does Luke keep his belongings?
In his sky-locker.

Why are people scared of the Empire?
They're a Boba Threat.

What do Jedi call a head cold? A mind-
sick.

What does Leia say to someone about to do a bad magazine cover? "Into the garbage shoot, flyboy."

Why was the droid acting so confidant? It R2-D-Knew everything.

How do the Gungans scare each other? "Na-Boo!"

How did Han teach Finn how to eat with chopsticks? He said, "That's not how the fork works."

What did the droid say when someone wanted to sell it for parts? C-3P-NO.

What do you call a Jedi wearing a winter hat? Toque Skywalker.

What's the dark side's favorite dinosaur? The Tyrannus.

Who judged a talent competition on the Death Star? Darth Raters.

What's Rey's favorite prehistoric animal? A light-sabre.

What does Mark Hamill call a fan that follows him around wherever he goes? A Luke Sky-stalker.

Who did Dana Carvey play in Star Wars? Garth Vader.

What do Jedi like to look at on the beach? Mind-chicks.

How does Ben Solo exercise? He Kylo runs.

Where do Rebels get their retriever puppies? Gold Breeder.

Why does Daisy Ridley go to church so often? She likes to p-Rey.

What did Han Solo say to the roulette dealer? "Never tell me the odds."

How do Jedi get around in the country? They use the horse.

Why was IT in Episode II? He thought it was Attack of the Clowns.

Where did Han Solo go to school? Stan-Ford.

What do dark-side, female Jedi get when they wear tight shoes? Night-blisters.

How do Senators stay healthy? They only eat Organa-c.

How did Chewbacca win the lottery? He was very Wookie.

Why did people think Carrie Fisher toyed with men's hearts? She was a p-Leia-er.

How did Anakin save the day in the pod race? He Pada-won.

How do Gungans transport large amounts of cash? In the Jar Jar Brinks truck.

What did Darth Vader say said to Luke after he chopped his hand off? "I am your Dad-awan."

Which Star Wars movie features dentists fighting on a frozen planet? The Empire Strikes Plaque.

How do Jedi open doors without the force? A Key-Adi-Mundi.

Which Star Wars character is best at swimming? Finn.

Why was Mark Hamill called the class clown? For being a Sky-mocker.

What do you call a Sith lord that eats a lot of potatoes? Darth Taters.

What does Han say when people are too chatty? "Great, kid. Don't get talky."

What do Rebel birds say to give a warning when they see storm troopers? Pana-kaw.

When is Natalie Portman is going to retire? When she's old and Pad-grey.

What did Han Solo say when they got to the ice planet? "Bring a jacket, Chewy, it's Hot-h outside."

Why was Padme annoying at times? She would get under people's Ana-skin.

What do you call a huge argument on the dark side? Making a Palpa-scene.

Why do droids believe in instead of destiny? BB-Fate.

Why does Mark Hamill like being electrocuted? He likes a good Sky-shocker.

What happens to the Empire when it rains? They get Boba Wet.

What do you call a rude Rebel? Boss Sass.

What do Jedi use instead of pepper spray? Mace Windu.

Why couldn't two Jedi get in touch? They were in Phone Wars.

Where does Natalie Portman swim? In the Pad-bay.

Which member of the dark side loves cigars? Supreme Leader Smoke.

What do Jedi say when offered dessert? "Yo, Duh."

How does the Dark Side know when the Jedi are about to attack? They have a sith-sense.

Which roller coaster would Darth Vader go on? The dark ride.

How do people know they're getting a good beer from the Rebellion? Because Harrison poured.

What kind of lizard does the dark side like for pets? Newt Gungrays.

How could you tell the droid was sad?
It looked R2-D-Blue.

Where do Storm Troopers take their
sick animals? The Boba Vet.

How do Senators leave the party early?
They Bail Organa-cally.

What do girl Jedi call their boyfriends?
Obi-Wan Keno-bae.

What did Ben Solo raise on the farm? A
Kylo hen.

What do you call Episode II in modern time? Attack of the Drones.

Why is there so much junk on the Millennium Falcon? Chewy is a Harrison Hoarder.

Why did Finn buy an iPhone? He lost his an-droid.

What does Yoda use to color his clothes? Jed-dye.

What's Anakin's favorite Asian dish? Padme-Thai.

What does a Wookie play in the casino? Chew-baccarat.

What's Natalie Portman's favorite month? Pad-may.

What do Star Wars characters tell their children when they eat? Chew-bacca and swallow.

What do you call someone in the First Order that goes bankrupt? Supreme Leader Broke.

What does Gwendoline Christie call her main show after working in Star Wars? Attack of the Thrones.

What does Luke Skywalker say when he kills his enemies? "Jed-die!"

How do Star Wars characters get place to place without a spaceship? On a Boba Jet.

What do you call an apprentice who becomes a Jedi? A grad-awan.

Which Wookie is best at classical music? Chew-bach-ah.

How do the Naboo cook their eggs? In a Captain Pan-aka.

How do Jedi play soccer? By doing mind-kicks.

How do Jedi get lids off jars? They use night-twisters.

Why are Wookies so difficult to ride? The don't stop Chew-buck-ing.

Who is the best Rebel rapper? Boss Nas.

What do you call male Jedi students? Lad-awans.

Which member of the Empire is the best to have at a party? Nute Fun-ray.

What's Darth Vader's favorite number? The four...ce.

Where does the Resistance get inked? Tatoo-ine.

What medicine do you give commanders injured on the field? Cody-ne.

How does Natalie Portman make sculptures? With Pad-clay.

What does Rey call her good bunkmates? Light-neighbors.

What do you call a Wookie that follows you around? A Chew-stalk-ah.

What does Han Solo say in early May? "May the fourth be with you."

What does Natalie Portman play with her children? Padme Cakes.

Why didn't the droid fit into the Jedi's robe? It was BB-over-weight.

What illness do a lot of droids catch? The R2-D-Flu.

Who's the worst person to be stuck in a spaceship with? Luke Sky-talker.

What did one droid who was falling behind say to the other? BB-Wait!

What did Han call Leia after they started dating? Princess Bae-ah.

How do Jedi light candles? With mind-wicks.

What doesn't Ben Solo use pencils? He prefers Kylo pens.

Which Tarantino movie do Star Wars characters love to watch? Django Fett.

What happens to Jango in the gym? He Boba Sweats.

Why did Anakin start going to the gym? To bcome Jedi Faster.

Why did the droid get kicked off the ship? He was C-creepy-O.

What do droids eat off of? A BB-Plate.

What to you call a chatty Wookie? Chew-talk-ah.

How is electricity measured on Tatooine? In Wattos.

How do people from the core worlds express their frustrations? "I Corus-can't even."

What would make Episode I twice as scary? The Tandem Menace.

Why is Mark Hamill great at volleyball? He's a great Sky-blocker

How does Han Solo always let his phone die? He keeps losing his Harrison Cord.

What do you call a shocked Wookie?
Chew-balk-ah.

What do people say when they leave
the swamp planet? "Dago-bye."

Who's the best dressed member of the
First Order? General Tux.

What's the easiest way to make a
droid angry? Push its buttons.

What do dark Jedi call a lightsaber that
looks like a sledgehammer? A darth
maul.

Who do you call if a dead Jedi is annoying you? The Force Ghostbusters.

Why don't people eat Wookies? The meat is too chewy.

Why can't Sand People do math? Because they always hide their numbers.

What is a Jedi's least favorite part of the Moon? The dark side.

What is the most popular website on Kashyyyk? Wookiepedia.

Where can you buy a robotic limb? At the secondhand store.

Why does Yoda have so many houseplants? He's got a green thumb.

Why should you never buy a used car from Darth Vader? Because he'll keep altering the deal.

Why does Darth Vader drive a Ford Mustang? Because the ability to destroy a planet is insignificant next to the power of the horse.

Which member of the dark side is the most politically correct? Supreme Leader Woke.

What do you call a droid that dies and turns into a ghost? See-Through-Pee-Oh.

CPSIA information can be obtained
at www.ICGtesting.com
Printed in the USA
BVHW032218181219
567165BV00002B/553/P

9 781696 728546